W9-BNP-174

SCIENCE AROUND US

Solids, Liquids, and Gases

By Darlene R. Stille

THE CHILD'S WORLD®
CHANHASSEN, MINNESOTA

The Child's World

Published in the United States of America by The Child's World®
PO Box 326, Chanhassen, MN 55317-0326
800-599-READ
www.childsworld.com

Content Adviser:
Mats Selen, PhD,
Professor of Physics,
University of Illinois,
Urbana, Illinois

Photo Credits: Cover: Paul A. Souders/Corbis. Interior: Corbis: 5, 9 (Michael Prince), 14, 23 (John Madere), 25 (Gerald Zanetti), 26 (Roger Ressmeyer); Custom Medical Stock Photo: 6; Getty Images: 20 (Photographer's Choice/Eduardo Garcia), 27 (David McNew), 30-middle (Hulton|Archive); Getty Images/Photodisc: 10, 16; Getty Images/Taxi: 17 (Aitch), 19 (Benelux); Hulton-Deutsch Collection/Corbis: 30-top, 30-bottom; Photo Researchers: 7 (Scott Camazine), 8 (Ted Kinsman), 11 (Laguna Design), 15 (Michael Bluestone), 18 (Charles D. Winters); PictureQuest: 13 (Creatas), 21 (David Chasey/Photodisc), 22 (Vincent DeWitt/Stock, Boston Inc.), 24 (Arthur Tilley/i2i Images); Rick Poley/Visuals Unlimited: 12.

The Child's World®: Mary Berendes, Publishing Director

Editorial Directions, Inc.: E. Russell Primm, Editorial Director; Pam Rosenberg, Line Editor; Katie Marsico, Assistant Editor; Matt Messbarger, Editorial Assistant; Susan Hindman, Copy Editor; Susan Ashley, Proofreader; Peter Garnham, Olivia Nellums, and Katherine Trickle, Fact Checkers; Tim Griffin/IndexServ, Indexer; Cian Laughlin O'Day, Photo Researcher; Linda S. Koutris, Photo Selector

The Design Lab: Kathleen Petelinsek, Design; Kari Thornborough, Page Production

Library of Congress Cataloging-in-Publication Data
Stille, Darlene R.
  Solids, liquids, and gases / by Darlene R. Stille.
    v. cm. — (Science around us)
  Includes bibliographical references and index.
  Contents: Discovering states of matter—Exploring solids—Exploring liquids—Exploring gases—Changing states—Using solids, liquids, and gases.
   ISBN 1-59296-225-4 (lib. bdg. : alk. paper) 1. Matter—Properties—Juvenile litera-ture. [1. Matter—Properties.] I. Title. II. Science around us (Child's World (Firm))
   QC173.36.S757 2005
   530.4—dc22   2003027362

TABLE OF CONTENTS

CHAPTER ONE

DISCOVERING STATES OF MATTER

People have probably always known a solid when they saw one. They could chop down solid trees. They could sit on solid rocks.

People have probably always known a liquid when they saw one. They could drink liquid milk from cows and goats. They could swim in liquid water.

People have always had gases all around them. They breathed in **air** made of gases. But people could not see these gases. So they did not know that gases were there.

Scientists in the 1600s began to think there might be something other than solids and liquids. A Belgian chemist named Jan Baptista van Helmont called this mysterious thing gas. *Gas* comes from a Greek word that means "space."

*You can swim through liquid water, but you would
not be able to swim through a solid or a gas.*

Scientists in the 1700s discovered many gases. They heated

certain kinds of solids or liquids in glass tubes. The heated material

gave off gases. They trapped the gases in the tubes. This is how the gases known as chlorine, hydrogen, and carbon dioxide were discovered.

An English minister and amateur scientist named Joseph Priestley made some of the most important discoveries about gases. He discovered

Antoine Lavoisier was born in Paris, France, in 1743. He became a scientist and made many important contributions in the field of chemistry.

oxygen. A French chemist named Antoine Lavoisier learned how to weigh gases. He also proved that oxygen is the gas necessary for respiration (or breathing) and combustion (or burning). All animals must breathe oxygen in order to live. Nothing will burn without oxygen.

Scientists later learned that solids, liquids, and gases are different types of **matter.** Matter is everything around you. Everything in the universe is made of matter.

Scientists call solids, liquids, and gases "states of matter." They know that all matter is made of tiny building blocks called **molecules.** They know that molecules are what make solids, liquids, and gases different from each other.

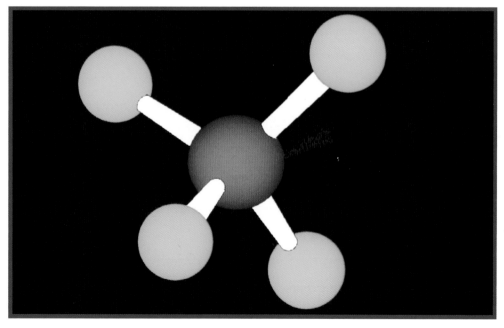

Models of molecules, such as this model of a methane gas molecule, can help us to understand what matter is made of.

BEAUTIFUL CRYSTALS

Crystals are a special type of solid. Crystals can have beautiful shapes. A diamond is a crystal.

Table salt is also a crystal. Pour a little salt on a plate or paper towel. Look closely at each grain of salt. Salt is made up of little cubes. Each cube is a crystal. Molecules in a crystal line up in a special way. They look a little like marching soldiers or a marching band.

Have you ever watched a marching band in a parade? All the musicians line up in rows. Each row has the same number of musicians. This is how molecules line up in a crystal. They are all in rows. The molecules in a crystal do not march. They stay in one place. They give the crystal its shape.

There are many kinds of crystals. Each kind has its own shape. **Metals** are made of crystals. Rocks are made of crystals. Beautiful snowflakes are made of crystals of ice.

CHAPTER TWO

EXPLORING SOLIDS

Look around. Try to find some solids. The chair you are sitting on is a solid. The floor you are standing on is a solid. Your table or desk is a solid. Brick walls and concrete sidewalks are solids. Almost everything around you is a solid.

This brick wall and door are examples of solid matter.

How can you tell when you see a solid? A solid always has its own shape. A solid does not change shape by itself.

You can change the shape of a solid if you work at it. You can saw a piece of wood in half. Each piece will still have its own shape.

You can pound a rock with a hammer. You can break the rock into tiny pieces. Each piece will still be a solid with its own shape.

A piece of metal wire is a solid. You can bend a wire into a new shape. The bent wire will still be a solid.

Scientists learned that solids have shape because of their molecules. Molecules in a solid are tightly packed. These molecules do not move around very much. They stay in one place.

You can use a pick to break a rock into many pieces. Each piece, no matter how small, will still be a solid with its own shape.

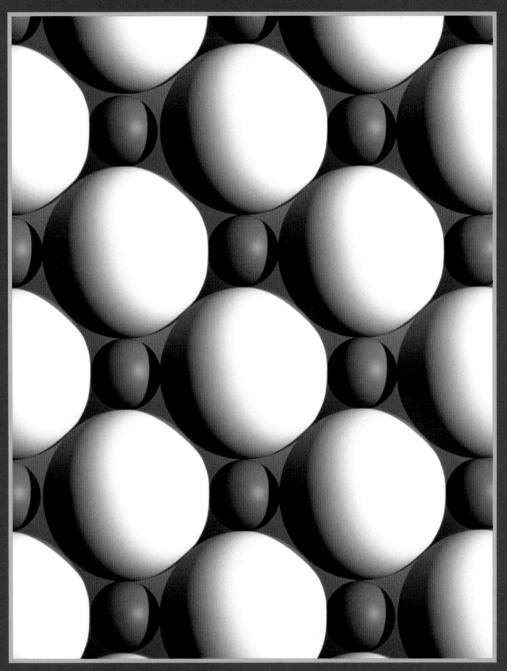

A model of the crystal structure of table salt shows how the molecules of a solid are tightly packed and do not move around.

CHAPTER THREE

EXPLORING LIQUIDS

Turn on a faucet and watch the water come out. Now put a glass under the faucet. Fill the glass with water. The water stays in the glass. The water has the shape of the glass.

Put some water in a pan. The water takes the shape of the pan.

Water is a liquid. A liquid does not have a shape of its own. A liquid takes the shape of any container it is in.

Water flowing from a faucet into a glass will take the shape of the glass.

Liquids also flow. You can pour water. Pour some water from the glass into a bowl. Watch how the water flows from the glass into the bowl. Take a look at the water in a river or stream. It keeps moving, or flowing.

Liquids flow and can be easily poured from one container into another.

There are many kinds of liquids. Milk is a liquid. Soda pop is a liquid. The syrup you pour on your pancakes is a liquid. Syrup does not flow as fast as water flows. Syrup is a thick liquid.

A liquid does not have shape, but it does have **volume.** Get a measuring cup. Measure out one cup of water. One cup is the volume of the water.

A container full of marbles can help you understand how the molecules of a liquid behave.

Pour the water into a bowl. Try not to spill it. Now pour the water back into the measuring cup. You still have one cup of water. The volume did not change when you poured water from one container into another. The way that molecules line up is what makes a liquid different from a solid. The molecules in a solid are tightly packed and are stuck together. They are kind of like a bunch of marbles that are glued to one another. They do not move much. The molecules in a liquid are also packed together tightly, but they are not stuck together. You can think of them like a bag full of marbles. They move around much more and can flow around each other. But they are still so close together that a liquid has its own volume.

CHAPTER FOUR

EXPLORING GASES

You cannot hold a gas in your hand. You cannot lean against a gas. You cannot pour a gas into a cup or bowl. Many gases are invisible. So how can you tell what a gas is?

Scientists say that a gas is something that expands, or goes out, to fill any size container. If you put a gas in a pickle jar, the gas will fill the pickle jar. If you

You can't see the air that you breathe out of your lungs, but if you blow the air into a balloon the balloon will expand to prove that the air is there.

Scientists in the 1700s used scales such as this to weigh gases.

put the same amount of gas in a huge tank, the gas will fill the tank.

A gas has no shape of its own. It has no volume of its own. But a gas does have **weight.** Remember that scientists in the 1700s learned how to weigh gases? First, they weighed a container without a gas in it. Then they trapped a gas in the container and weighed the container with the gas inside. The difference between the two weights was the weight of the gas.

Molecules in gases zoom all around. They go every which way. They keep zooming outward until they bounce off a wall. This is how they expand to fill any size container they are in. This zooming around is why a gas does not have a volume of its own.

CHAPTER FIVE

FROM SOLID TO LIQUID TO GAS

S olid, liquid, and gas are three different states of matter. Many

kinds of matter can change states. A solid can change to a

liquid. A liquid can change to a gas.

There are two basic ways to change a material's state of matter.

You can change its temperature. You can make something hotter or

A thermometer can be used to measure the temperature of a solid, liquid, or gas.

Nitrogen (being poured, above) is normally found as a gas, but it will become a liquid at very cold temperatures.

colder. You can change the

pressure of a gas. Gas pres-

sure is just the force of mole-

cules banging against a

container wall. You can

squeeze the molecules more

tightly together. You can let

the molecules get farther apart.

Let's use ordinary water

to see how temperature can

change states of matter.

Water is normally a liquid.

But water can change into

a solid or a gas.

At room temperature, water is found in the liquid state.

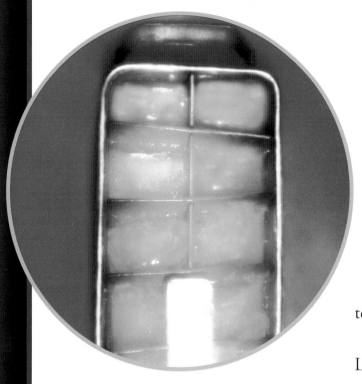

Water becomes a solid at 0° Celsius (32° Fahrenheit). Ice is solid water.

Let's change a liquid to a solid. Fill an ice cube tray with liquid water. Put the tray in your freezer. It is very cold in the freezer. The cold lowers the temperature of the water. Lowering the temperature makes the water molecules slow down. When the water gets cold enough, the water molecules slow down enough to make a solid. Liquid water freezes into solid ice.

This change happens at 0°Celsius (32°Fahrenheit). This temperature is called the **freezing point** of water. Above 0°C (32°F), ice starts to melt. Solid ice turns back into a liquid. So 0°C (32°F) is also called the **melting point** of ice.

Let's change a liquid to a gas. Pour some water into a pot. Have a grown-up help you put the pot on a stove. Turn on the heat. Heat from the stove raises the temperature of the water. Heat makes the liquid molecules move faster and faster. Suddenly, they are moving fast enough to fly up in the air. The liquid water is hot

The heat from a stove makes the molecules of liquid move faster and faster. When the molecules are moving fast enough, the substance being heated will become a gas.

Water boils at 100°C (212°F).

enough to turn into a gas. You can see steam—tiny droplets of water—

going into the air above the pot. The steam is called water vapor.

Liquid water changes into a gas at 100°C (212°F) . This tempera-

ture is called the **boiling point** of water.

MELTING POINTS AND BOILING POINTS

Ice begins to melt above 0°C (32°F). Other materials have different melting points. Some melting points are much higher. Tungsten is a metal that has a very high melting point. It changes from a solid to a liquid at about about 6,100°C (3,370°F).

Iron is a metal that is normally a solid. At about 1,535°C (2,795°F), iron becomes a red-hot liquid. Big furnaces in **foundries** melt iron. Workers pour the liquid iron into molds. The iron becomes a solid again when it cools. This is how iron is molded into frying pans, fences, patio furniture, automobile parts, and other products.

Water boils at about 100°C (212°F). Other materials have different boiling points. Some of these points are very cold. Helium changes from a liquid to a gas at about –269°C (–452°F). No wonder helium is normally a gas!

CHAPTER SIX

USING SOLIDS, LIQUIDS, AND GASES

t is a good thing that there are different states of matter.

You can nail wooden boards together to build a house.

You can bolt metal plates together to make an ocean liner.

Wooden boards are often used to build houses. Solids make good building materials.

HAMBURGERS AND LIQUID GAS

Do you like hamburgers cooked on a grill? You can grill hamburgers over a charcoal fire. You can also cook hamburgers on a gas grill.

Gas grills use a special kind of fuel called propane. Propane is normally a gas and is made from oil or petroleum. Propane normally expands to fill the container it is in. But the propane you buy for a gas grill is actually a liquid.

"Squeezing" the propane into small tanks or metal bottles changed it from a gas to a liquid. Squeezing the propane made the gas molecules come closer together. The closer the molecules came, the less they could move around. When the molecules came close enough, the propane turned into a liquid.

A hose hooks the propane tank up to the barbecue grill. Turning on the grill makes some propane shoot out of the tank. Outside the tank, the molecules can zoom around again, and the propane turns back into a gas. The gas starts to burn when it hits the flame on the grill. Now get ready to grill some burgers!

Imagine trying to nail two puddles of water together. Imagine trying to fasten globs of air together with bolts. You can drink a cup of milk or a can of soda pop. You

You can drink milk and other liquids through a curly straw.

could never drink a rock. You can breathe air into your lungs.

You could never breathe a bush or a tree. Solids, liquids, and

gases are so important in our world. We need all the different

states of matter in order to live.

*Heating up air to make its molecules move faster and faster
makes these beautiful hot air balloons fly high in the sky.*

GLOSSARY

air (AIR) Air is the invisible mixture of gases that surrounds Earth.

boiling point (BOYL-ing POINT) The temperature at which a liquid turns into a gas is its boiling point.

foundries (FOUN-drees) Foundries are factories for melting down metals and molding them into different shapes.

freezing point (FREEZ-ing POINT) The temperature at which a liquid turns into a solid is its freezing point.

matter (MAT-ur) Matter is anything in the universe that takes up space and has weight.

melting point (MELT-ing POINT) The temperature at which a solid turns into a liquid is its melting point.

metals (MET-uhls) Metals are materials, such as iron or copper, that are usually hard and shiny and are good conductors of electricity and heat.

molecules (MOL-eh-kyools) Molecules are the smallest bits of a material that still have all of the characteristics of that material.

oxygen (OK-seh-juhn) Oxygen is a gas found in the air that all humans and animals need to breathe.

pressure (PRESH-ur) Pressure is the force of something pressing on a container.

volume (VOL-yuhm) The amount of space that something fills is its volume.

weight (WAYT) Weight is the measure of the pull of gravity on an object.

DID YOU KNOW?

▶ English minister and scientist Joseph Priestley invented soda water in the 1700s. He ran a gas called carbon dioxide through water. Adding this gas makes soda pop and other carbonated drinks.

▶ The pull of Earth's gravity holds the gases in air in place around Earth. Gravity is strong close to the ground. Higher up, gravity is weaker.

▶ Birthday balloons float in the air because they are filled with a gas called helium. Helium weighs less than air. Balloons filled with lighter helium float up through the heavier air.

▶ Most solids shrink when they get colder. Ice is odd. Ice expands or gets bigger.

▶ Hot air is lighter than cold air. Hot air makes colorful hot-air balloons float in the sky. Fire under a balloon heats the air trapped inside the balloon, making the balloon rise.

▶ It's hard to squeeze solids and liquids. Their molecules are already close together. It's easy to squeeze gases because their molecules are far apart.

▶ Electricity can turn some gases into a state called a plasma. Neon signs are made of glass tubes filled with neon gas. Electricity going through the tubes turns neon into a plasma and makes it glow.

▶ Some gases have color. A gas called nitrogen dioxide is brown. Some gases have a smell. A gas called hydrogen sulfide smells like rotten eggs. Chlorine gas is yellowish green and has a strong, bad smell.

▶ An English scientist named Michael Faraday was one of the first people to study changing a gas into a liquid. He turned chlorine gas into a liquid in 1823.

▶ All snow crystals have six sides. Snow crystals stick together to make snowflakes.

TIMELINE

circa 400 B.C. Greek philosopher Democritus comes up with the theory that all matter is made up of particles that cannot be broken down, or atoms.

early 1600s Scientists begin to understand that some matter can exist in a form that is similar to air.

mid-1600s Jan Baptista van Helmont (top left), a Belgian chemist, is the first person to use the word *gas* to describe this mysterious matter.

1755 Joseph Black discovers carbon dioxide, a gas.

1774 Joseph Priestley discovers oxygen.

1808 Scientist John Dalton (right) develops his atomic theory, which becomes the basis of all modern atomic science.

1811 Amadeo Avogadro demonstrates the relationship between the volume of a substance and the number of molecules it contains.

1823 Michael Faraday (left) turns chlorine gas into a liquid. His experiment is the first successful attempt to liquefy a gas.

HOW TO LEARN MORE ABOUT
SOLIDS, LIQUIDS, AND GASES

At the Library

Hewitt, Sally. *Solid, Liquid, or Gas?* New York: Children's Press, 1998.

Royston, Angela. *Solids, Liquids, and Gases.* Chicago: Heinemann Library, 2001.

Snedden, Robert. *States of Matter.* Chicago: Heinemann Library, 2001.

Zoehfeld, Kathleen Weidner, and Paul Meisel (illustrator). *What Is the World Made Of? All about Solids, Liquids, and Gases.* New York: HarperTrophy, 1998.

On the Web

VISIT OUR HOME PAGE FOR LOTS OF LINKS ABOUT SOLIDS, LIQUIDS, AND GASES:
http://www.childsworld.com/links.html
Note to Parents, Teachers, and Librarians: We routinely verify our Web links to make sure they're safe, active sites—so encourage your readers to check them out!

Places to Visit or Contact

THE EXPLORATORIUM
To tour the exhibit on matter
3601 Lyon Street
San Francisco, CA 94123
415/397-5673

MIAMI MUSEUM OF SCIENCE
To see the Atoms Family exhibit
3280 South Miami Avenue
Miami, FL 33129
305/646-4200

INDEX

About the Author

Darlene R. Stille is a science writer. She has lived in Chicago, Illinois, all her life. When she was in high school, she fell in love with science. While attending the University of Illinois she discovered that she also loved writing. She was fortunate to find a career that allowed her to combine both her interests. Darlene Stille has written more than 60 books for young people.